Vernon L. Anley

Proverse Hong Kong
2024

The poems in THE WATER GARDEN fall into two main categories. Some are a personal response to prophetic utterances in the Old and New Testaments of the Christian Bible. Others derive from the observation and attention given to "particulate things and experiences". They give a sense of the poet's focus on the creative works of others, writers such as Keats and Wordsworth and Chuang Tzu, holocaust survivor Elie Wiesel, philosopher Wittgenstein, Christian mystic Jacob Boehme, sociologist Max Weber, and painters Edward Hopper, Georges Seurat, Renoir and of course Monet, whose painting, "The Water Garden at Giverny", from his Water Lilies series is significantly referenced in the title of Anley's collection. We find here also responses to the lyrics of popular, folk and traditional songs and to the art of Australian aborigine people.

VERNON L ANLEY was educated in Australia and England. After leaving university he worked with the Ministry of Overseas development in the West Indies before resuming an academic career in Europe and the Far East. He has co-authored and edited a number of books, written guides on the Hejaz and Yemen, and published novels, short stories and poetry. His novel, *A Carnival of Lies*, about the complex developments in Germany between 1939 and 1945, is considered a major work of historical fiction. Among his most recent publications, *An Unholy Love* takes the reader on a spiritual odyssey that transcends religious speculation in its apprehension of the imperishable power of love.

]

THE WATER GARDEN

AND

OTHER POEMS

Vernon L. Anley

Proverse Hong Kong

The Water Garden and Other Poems
By Vernon L. Anley

First published in Hong Kong by Proverse Hong Kong
under sole and exclusive right and licence,
July 2024.
Paperback edition: ISBN-13: 978-988-8833-91-7
Ebook edition: ISBN-13: 978-988-8833-92-4

Distribution (Hong Kong and worldwide)
The Chinese University of Hong Kong Press,
The Chinese University of Hong Kong,
Shatin, New Territories, Hong Kong SAR.
Email: cup@cuhk.edu.hk; Web: www.cup.cuhk.edu.hk
Distribution (United Kingdom)
Stephen Inman, Worcester, UK.
Enquiries to Proverse Hong Kong
P.O. Box 259, Tung Chung Post Office,
Lantau, NT, Hong Kong SAR, China.
Email: proverse@netvigator.com;
Web: www.proversepublishing.com

The right of Vernon L. Anley to be identified as the author of this work
has been asserted by him in accordance with
the Copyright, Designs and Patents Act 1988.

Author photo, courtesy the Author

Cover image: Bee Taplin

British Library Cataloguing in Publication Data
A catalogue record for the first paperback edition
is available from the British Library

PRIOR PUBLICATION ACKNOWLEDGEMENTS

Several poems, previously published by Wipf and Stock Publishers in *Selected Poems,* are included in *The Water Garden* because they belong to a small group of religious-oriented poems which are included in this collection. For the rest, all the poems are new to this anthology.

OTHER TITLES BY VERNON L. ANLEY

A Carnival of Lies (Novel)
An Unholy Love (Novel)
A Divided Universe (Novel)
It Happened in Hanoi (Novel)
The Orange Tree and Other Stories
The Last Song (Poetry)
Selected Poems

CONTENTS

INTRODUCTION

I have found biblical texts a particularly rich source of material for poetry because of their evocative use of language and imagery and mystical accounts of salvation. I have not attempted to clarify the succinct utterances of prophetic speech, or interpret the eschatological visions found in the Old and New Testaments. I do not regard myself as either a preacher or a theologian, even if the language I use may sometimes suggest that I hope to be both. The poems in this collection that have a biblical reference are simply a personal response to what I have read and what I have understood.

When Rilke complained to Rodin that he lacked inspiration Rodin replied, "Why don't you just go and look at something – for example, an animal in the Jardin des Plantes, and keep on looking at it until you're able to make a poem of it?" Rilke took Rodin's advice. The poems in this collection, apart from those with a biblical reference, are likewise the result of "observation and attention" (Rilke). However only at the beginning is the poet ruled by purpose. Everything beyond that is involuntary, allowing his vision by way of a mysterious interaction of meanings conveyed by the sentences to give form to experiences that continually bring one up against the limitations of language.

Vernon L. Anley
April 2024

POEMS

I SAW THE SPIRIT DESCENDING FROM HEAVEN LIKE A DOVE

"I saw the Spirit descending from heaven like a dove"
   —John 1:32

There is a notable anonymity about the Spirit

Like the wind it blows where it will

You hear the sound of it

But you do not know from whence it comes

Or where it goes.

It is not the product of our will or choice

It reaches beyond itself

Diminishing the horizon

That sets a limit to our knowing

And opens our hearts

To a new level of being.

HOW DOES A POEM COME TO BE

"Some kind of feeling now within myself should be
commencing."
>   —**Rilke**

How does a poem come to be?

From imagination and from dream

And feeling things silently

Through inwardness and through outwardness

A poem comes to be.

I TOOK FRIGHT

"I took fright, realising that I could not turn back, so
I went ahead, urged forward by a force that is quite
alien to my normal life as a man."
  —Matisse

ɪnspɪˈreɪʃn/, inspirare, inspirarion

A restless creative spirit that summons the artist

And makes him his instrument.

There is a notable anonymity to this gift of the spirit.

Like the Johanine pneuma it blows where it wills

You hear the sound of it

But you do not know from whence it comes

In itself it is wordless and imageless:

But finds expression in the artist's work.

AUSTRALIA IS WAITING FOR THE POET

Australia is waiting for the poet

To paint in words

The landscape of its artists:

The parched ochre of ancient flood plains

The excessive spaces of the Outback

The windswept ranges and deserts

Where local spirits laid song lines

And the soul's geographer

Brought dreaming to a land

Laid bare by time.

THE LOOMING TREE

Look! see how far apart they sit
The couple on the park bench
Facing the looming tree
That hides the gardens
The colourful flower beds
The children playing
And people enjoying the sunshine.

But this happy scene is hidden from our couple
By the looming tree
That separates them from the gardens
The colourful flower beds
People enjoying the sunshine
And children's laughter.

If our couple would speak to one another
Or turn to one another
And accept each other's presence
They could enjoy the gardens and flowers
The sunshine and children's laughter
And ignore the looming tree
That keeps them apart

GOD REVEALS HIMSELF TO MOSES

God reveals himself to Moses with the expression, "I
Am Who I Am."
      —Exodus 3.

Man affirms God

And obscurely he knows what he means

As best he can expresses his meaning

But his resources for expression are unequal to the
task

He can give God a name,

But there are many tongues

And so there are many names

He can indicate God by analogy

But his analogies are imperfect reflections

To make God a cause is to consign him to the past

To make him an end is to postpone him to the future

To insist on his presence

Is to involve him in our affairs.

For all their usefulness

Our descriptions fall short of God's own self-
revelation

In Deuteron-Isaiah God spoke to the nations of the
world

Where he made the great claim:

I alone am God

The creator of all.

Before me there was no God, neither shall there be
after me.

Yea, before the day was I am he;

I alone am Yahweh, and apart from me there is no
other

For I am the LORD thy God, and thy saviour.

MR WITTGENSTEIN

"What can be said at all can be said clearly without
invention and whereof one cannot speak thereof one
must be silent."
—Ludwig Wittgenstein

Mr Wittgenstein,

Have you never been in love?

Have you never found the words to say

When your heart soars above the world

And you experienced a joy

You never imagined or expected to find.

Mr Wittgenstein,

Have you never come face to face with beauty?

Have you never felt the effect of great art

Upon your spirit

Elevating your feelings

Into a realm we do nothing to arrange

But which fills you with quiet joy.

Mr Wittgenstein,

Have you never ever gazed into the night sky

Ablaze with stars

And felt an unseen something.

A mysterium magnum

That leaves you breathless with wonder and with awe.

Dear Mr. Wittgenstein

Beside the gifts of the head

There are those of the heart.

When out for certainties in this life

What soulless answers we get

If we rely only on facts.

MONET'S WATER GARDEN

Stirred by the sole suggestion of a breeze.

Monet's water garden at Giverny

Mirrors with reflective ease

The floating colours of autumn.

The poet would paint the garden as Monet saw it.

The scattered radiance of blues and greens

And feather-pink flowers

So admired by Cezanne and Caillebotte

But rhyme is far afield from heaven's brush

To paint autumn's golden hour

When the hearts of flowers on the air are born

And colours mingle in one dream of light.

"NIGHTHAWKS"

(Title of a painting by Edward Hopper)

Midnight has long passed.

The city sleeps

Unaware of the couple in the corner café.

They sit together

Bathed in the faded glare of a neon light

That falls sparingly into the café

Our couple are mindless of each other

Staring beyond themselves

Perhaps they have exhausted

All that there was between them

Their life together has become an echo in memory

An echo that has lost its voice

Time has nothing to offer

It is best forgotten

Something tells me that that they are denizens of the

corner café

Comforted by the anonymity of empty tables

And the pallid glare of a neon light

Soon it will be dawn.

Sunrise will awaken the city

The streets will quicken with activity

And our couple will make their way home

Perhaps to sleep, perhaps to dream

Who knows?

Until night falls

And takes them back to the corner café.

AND WHAT, DEAR GOD?

"But the day of the Lord will come like a thief, and
then the heavens will pass away with a roar, and the
earth and all the works that are done on it will be
destroyed."
        —2 Peter

And what, dear God, of beauty

When the world is brought to an end?

The sun's wrath will fall upon the earth

Destroying all man's work

The riches of art, of music, of literature

The touchstones of the human spirit

Will become as dust and ashes in the conflagration

But if beauty's resonance

Is born of the human spirit

Its fruits are carried into eternal memory

Thereby affirming the value of man's work

For the divine life and its eternal glory.

PEACE I LEAVE WITH YOU

"The dead shall live. Their bodies rise."
—**Isaiah**

Peace I leave with you.

My peace, I give you.

Do not fear

Or let your hearts be troubled.

I have called you by your name

You are mine.

Neither darkness nor death

Will stand in your way

I am your salvation

You shall know my love

And abide with me

For all eternity

Unmagical!

Unmystical, unspeculative even

A divine self giving and alliance of love

That brings man to God.

I SAW MY CORPSE

"Auschwitz means death, total absolute death – of man and all people, of language and imagination, of time and spirit."
>   **—Elie Wiesel**

I saw my corpse among the dead

My charred bones among the ashes

My broken skull among the skeletons

God help us!

You fall down

You die

Deliverance and salvation

Are no more

Standing before the Gates of Hell

My soul vexed unto death

I cry out:

Eli, Eli, lama sabachthani?

My God, my God, why hast thou forsaken me?

CLOUDS ARE ROLLING LIKE WAVES

Clouds are rolling like waves over the Criou
When the storm breaks
Shoppers will shelter behind beaded curtains
In the Bar de Savoie
And mad dog Toto
Whose happiness is barking at strangers
Will run indoors

When the rain stops
The clouds over the Criou will be forgotten
People will go about their business
In the Place du Gros-Tilleul
And mad dog Toto
Watchful as ever
Will bark again.

All that holds the memory
Of the clouds rolling over the Criou
The Bar de Savoie with its beaded curtains
The shoppers in the Place du Gros-Tilleul
And mad dog Toto
Are these lines of verse uttered in passing.

THE DREAM GOES ON FOREVER

"The mystic death is the beginning of eternal life."
 —Jacob Boehme

The dream goes on forever.

Only the dreamers die.

Past reasons last endeavour.

Beliefs lost ecstasy.

LET US GO A-WALKING

Let us go a-walking
Along woodland's golden paths
Our hands a-touching
Lost in that floating world of dream
Where sorrow falls away
And time might scarcely be.
Ah my sweet!
Let us go a-walking
Far from fevered human hours
In meadows fervent with appeal
Where love and hope
Know nothing more than the unheeding flowers
Need know their own beauty's law.

WHY IN SUCH SPIRITLESS TIMES?

Who shall I tell my sorrow?
My despair greener than ice.
Angels look on aghast at what they see.
A world distraught with suffering and sorrow
Why, in such spiritless times
Be a poet at all?

Who shall I tell my sorrow?
My despair greener than ice.

Soon all of us will sleep under the Earth.
We who never let each other sleep above it
Why linger then
And not know what to begin or to utter?

The Water Garden

MAN ENTERS THE WORLD

"The LORD my God will enlighten my darkness."
—Psalm 18:28

Man enters the world with a cry

Yet there is reason to rejoice

For after this life

God himself is our place.

Most assuredly I tell you

The hidden things of darkness

Will be revealed and brought to light

For he is the light of the world

And in him there is no darkness at all.

LA GUITARRA

(Title of a Song by Los Auténticos Decadentes, released 1995)

La guitarra

Desgrans notas

Que son garras

En penas remotas

From the guitar

You draw notes

That fall like arrows

On pains I had forgotten.

WE LIVE IN TWO WORLDS

"We live in two worlds: the world of daily life that operates in standard time and standard space and the world of our imagination."
—Max Weber

The Daoist teacher Chuang Tzu

Dreamt he was a butterfly

Fluttering about

Happily doing as he pleased

He didn't know if he was Chuang Tzu

Or somebody else

For he was in a different world

When woken suddenly

There he was

 n his own body

Solid and unmistakably Chuang Tzu

But he didn't know if he was Chuang Tzu

Who dreamt he was a butterfly

Or a butterfly

Dreaming he was Chuang Tzu.

YOU TURN AWAY

You turn away
And show your disgust
At my unkempt hair
My ragged clothes and broken nails.

Your pretty dress
Your pearl earrings
Hide what you are
What I am
What we are

When death takes us
Between silk sheets
Or alleyways
With blessings
Or without

We will know ourselves
As we truly are
Not 'I' and not 'You'
But one in being
In spirit and in love.

LOVERS

Look, lovers
See how they come towards us
Through the flowering grass
And slowly
Their whole heart
So engaged
They find no words to speak
And time might scarcely be.

THE ORANGE TREE

Be quiet
The young girl said.
Can't you see
I'm listening to the Orange tree.
I hear no voice.
It's an enchanted tree.
The young girl said.
A light not of the sky.
Lives in the Orange tree.
I see no light.
You do not see what I can see.
Let me be.
So I may listen to the Orange tree.
I hear no voice.
There is no voice the young girl said.
But it is almost sound
And it falls from the Orange Tree.
What does it say? I asked.
It tells of a time when the earth was young
And man could do no wrong.
Animals had learned to speak
And birds to sing to him.

I hear no voice and see no light

Your heart is empty.

The young girl said

Without love you will not see what I can see

The light that lives in the Orange Tree.

LOVE HAS NO CURE

"Se volvieron a encontar
Al revolver una esquina
Y como des criaturas
Se pusieron a lloar
El amor no tiene cura."

—Cante Flamenco

They rounded a corner
And met again
And like two children
Began to cry
Love has no cure.

KUR-ING-GAI

Kur-ing-gai
Home of the Kuringgai people
Whose paintings and song lines
Trace the paths of creator beings
Who sang the world into existence
And made everything beautiful.

Born of a knowledge from within
For God set the world in their heart
The Kuringgai divine God's nature
Through all he has made
And created.

Pilgrim man
A stranger to the vision of God
Must wait for the appointed time
When the invisible things of him
From the creation of the world are seen
And understood by the things that are made.

KEATS AND WORDSWORTH

Keats and Wordsworth
And other great poets
Speak to us from natural necessity
In words that reveal
The spiritual activity behind reality.
We whose verse
Reflects the occasional and the transitory
And whose hearts
Are tied to its own concerns
Can take comfort from Theocritus' words
To the young poet Eumenes
Who after struggling for two years
Managed to write only one idyll;

And if you are on the first step
You ought to be proud and pleased.
Coming as far as this is not little
What you have achieved deserves great praise
For even this first step
Is far distant from the common lot
To set your foot upon this step.
You must rightfully be a citizen

Of the city of ideas

And in that city it is hard

And rare to be naturalised

Coming as far as this is not little

What you achieved is great glory.

SEURAT HAS UNROLLED HIS CANVAS:
"A SUNDAY ON LA GRANDE JATTE"

(Title of an 1884 painting by Georges Seurat)

Seurat has unrolled his canvas in Russell Square
Allowing the Parisians
To step out of his painting and join us.

You must admit it's a beautiful day.
The sky is an unbroken curve of stainless blue.
And the mid afternoon sunlight
Bathes the gardens in an afternoon glow.

You would expect Seurat's Parisians
To talk among themselves
And gesture at things that catch their eye
Or at very least
To show some pleasure in their surroundings.

But the impression you will agree
Is one of absolute stillness
As if time had stood still and become frozen.

Take the fashionable couple with the dog.

The man elegantly dressed in top hat and silk cravat

Is as motionless as a figure on a marble frieze.

And his wife, certainly a femme de mode

In her stylish coat and fur collar

Is just as still and silent.

Seurat has us see our companions

As strangers to themselves

And to each other

Inhabiting a world that is not rightly theirs

And to which they do not belong.

Are we like Seurat's wealthy Parisians

Mute players in the drama of living

The setting is beautiful

The lighting is superb

The costume's gorgeous

But wherefore the play?

MR RENOIR

"White does not exist in nature."
—Renoir in conversation with a young artist
in 1910.

Mr. Renoir

Have you never stood and gazed

At a sky so white

That it dazzles the eye?

Or seen the snow white clouds

That float like ships upon the sea?

Have you never stopped to look

At a landscape covered in snow

As if with swathes of white satin?

Mr. Renoir have you looked with delight

At night blooming jasmine

Whose white flowers reflect the moon's light

And glow as white as opal.

Colours, Mr. Renoir

Are not ordained by the artist's pallet

Or the writers pen

But man's vision of heaven's beauty.

COMMENTS

Anley's poetry is remarkable for its delicacy and beautifully crafted verse. It springs from a pure source, working through intuition and feeling and what Plato called "the further side of being". His poems reveal a sense of the inexhaustible richness of nature and the immense value of just looking steadily at things without prejudice or preconception, patiently waiting for them to yield up their mysteries.

> —**Saskia McCallum**, high school teacher,
> formerly employed by the New South Wales
> Education Department

Anley's poems always have a definite and discoverable meaning. Although they often point beyond themselves, they are symbolic only in a sense of being evocative of particulate things and experiences. They can be read and reread with increasing pleasure.

> —**J.L. Moore**, filmmaker, specialized in
> making films about alternative schools and
> educational change

POETRY

PUBLISHED BY PROVERSE HONG KONG

Single author collections

Vinita Agrawal. *Twilight Language*. 2022.

Gillian Bickley. *China suite and other poems*. 2009.
———*For the record and other poems of Hong Kong*. 2003.
———*Grandfather's Robin*. 2020.
———*Moving house and other poems from Hong Kong*. 2005.
———*Sightings: a collection of poetry, with an essay, 'communicating poems'*. 2007.
———*Over the Years: Selected Collected Poems, 1972-2015*. 2017.
———*Perceptions*. 2012.

Liam Blackford. *A Gateway Has Opened*. 2021.

Paola Caronni. *Uncharted Waters*. 2021.

Celia Claase. *The layers between* (essays and poems). 2015.

Sally Dellow. *Wonder, lust & itchy feet*. 2011.

Ahmed Elbeshlawy. *Savage Charm*. 2019.

Andrew S. Guthrie. *Alphabet*, by. 2015.

D.J. Hamilton. *The Hummingbird Sometimes Flies Backwards*. 2019.

Jonathan Locke Hart. *The Burning Lake*. 2016.

Patty Ho. *Heart to Heart: Poems*. 2010.
——*Of leaves & ashes*, by 2016.

Henrik Hoeg. *Irreverent poems for pretentious people*. 2016.

Carolina Ilica. *Violet*. 2019.

L.W. Illsley. *Astra and Sebastian*. 2011.

Akin Jeje (Akinsola Olufemi Jeje). *Smoked pearl: poems of Hong Kong and beyond*. 2010.

Birgit Bunzel Linder. *Bliss of Bewilderment*. 2017.
——*Shadows in deferment*. 2013.

J.P. Linstroth. *Epochal Reckonings*. 2020.

Elbert Siu Ping Lee. *Rain on the pacific coast*. 2013.

Lelawattee Manoo-Rahming. *Immortelle and bhandaaraa poems*. 2011.

Marta Markoska. *Black Holes Within Us*. 2021.
——H/ERO/T/IC BOOK, 2020.

Jack Mayer. *Entanglements: Physics, love, and wilderness dreams*. 2022.
——*Poems from the Wilderness*. 2020.

Patricia Glinton Meicholas. *Chasing light*. 2013.

Vishal Nanda. *Please Stand Back from the Platform Door*. 2021.

Mary-Jane Newton. *Of symbols misused*. 2011.
——*Unlocking*. March 2014.

Jon Ng. *Hong Kong Growing Pains.* 2020.

James Norcliffe. *Shadow play.* 2012.

Nikhil Parekh. *Seeking Solace.* 2022.

Jason S. Polley. *Refrain.* 2010.

Vaughan Rapatahana. *Home, away, elsewhere..* 2011.

Kate Rogers. *Painting the borrowed house: poems.* 2008.

José Manuel Sevilla *The Year of the Apparitions.* 2020.

Shahilla Shariff. *Life Lines.* 2011.

Hayley Ann Solomon. *Celestial Promise.* 2017.

Laura Solomon. *Frida Kahlo's cry and other poems* 2015.
———*In vitro,* 2nd ed. 2014.

Shifting sands Deepa Vanjani. 2016.

Anthologies

Gillian and Verner Bickley, Editors. *Mingled voices: the international Proverse Poetry Prize anthology 2016-2023.* 2017-2024.

FIND OUT MORE ABOUT PROVERSE AUTHORS, BOOKS, EVENTS AND LITERARY PRIZES

Visit our website: https://www.proversepublishers.com
See the Proverse page on the CUHKP website:
https://cup.cuhk.edu.hk/Proversehk

Follow us on Twitter: twitter.com/Proversebooks
"Like" us on www.facebook.com/ProversePress
Subscribe to our Youtube channel:
youtube.com/@ProversePublishing

Request our free E-Newsletter
Send your request to info@proversepublishing.com

Availability
Available in Hong Kong and world-wide
from our Hong Kong based distributor,
the Chinese University of Hong Kong Press,
https://cup.cuhk.edu.hk/Proversehk
Most titles can be ordered online from amazon
(various countries).

Stock-holding retailers
Hong Kong (CUHKP, Bookazine)
Canada (Elizabeth Campbell Books),
Andorra (Llibreria La Puça, La Llibreria).
Orders may be made from bookshops
in the UK and elsewhere.

Ebooks and Audiobooks
Most of our paperback and hardback titles are available
also as Ebooks.
An increasing number of our titles are available as
audiobooks.

Printed in Great Britain
by Amazon

43381569R00030